FROM BARRACKS TO BOARDROOM

THE VETERAN'S GUIDE TO ENTREPRENEURSHIP

**BUILD YOUR OWN MISSION
AFTER THE MILITARY**

ASK ANTWAUN

From Barracks to Boardroom

The Veteran's Guide To Entrepreneurship

ISBN: 979-8-9936505-4-8

Published by AskAntwaun Media

All inquiries: AskAntwaun@gmail.com
Printed in the United States of America

Book Design by Williams DocuPrep
www.williamsdocuprep.com

Table of Contents

Acknowledgements

To every service member, veteran, and family who's ever wondered if financial freedom was really possible, this is for you. You've sacrificed, served, and endured. You deserve more than stability; you deserve prosperity.

To the agents, lenders, and mentors who continue to serve our military community through education and integrity, thank you. You make the difference between a buyer and a believer.

And to my family, for your patience, support, and faith during every late night, long call, and new project, you're the "why" behind every word.

Introduction

A New Mission Begins

When you leave the military, they'll tell you that your mission is over. They'll thank you for your service, hand you a DD-214, and send you back into a world that doesn't run on formation times, after-action reviews, or clear objectives. But what if I told you your next mission is the most important one yet—*and you're already trained for it?*

Entrepreneurship is the veteran's natural battlefield. Think about it: the same qualities that made you effective in uniform discipline, adaptability, leadership, and the ability to execute under pressure are the exact traits that make entrepreneurs unstoppable.

You already know how to build systems. You already know how to lead people. You already know how to improvise when the plan falls apart. That's business.

When I transitioned out of service, I thought I was done leading missions. What I didn't realize was that I had simply changed the terrain. The mission didn't end; it evolved. My uniform turned into a brand. My chain of command became my network. And my orders? They became goals I wrote myself.

This book is about turning that same military mindset into your entrepreneurial edge. You'll learn how to identify your purpose, build your business structure, leverage your resources, and create systems that give you both freedom and fulfillment. Whether you want to start a side hustle, scale a company, or build something that outlives your service, the path begins here with clarity, courage, and command. Because entrepreneurship isn't about starting a business. It's about taking ownership of your mission again.

Your service prepared you to follow orders. Now it's time to write your own.

Chapter 1

The Veteran Advantage

When I first left the Army, I thought I was starting from scratch. No uniform. No rank. No command structure. I felt like I'd been dropped into civilian life with a résumé full of leadership but no map.

But it didn't take long to realize something powerful. I wasn't starting over; I was starting ahead. The same skills that made me successful in the military were the exact ones entrepreneurs spend years trying to learn.

In the military, we're trained to think in systems. We plan, we adapt, and we execute under pressure. We know how to lead teams, manage chaos, and hit objectives no matter the odds. That's not just experience; that's an entrepreneurial mindset.

The problem is most of us don't recognize it. We underestimate what we already know because we were taught to focus on the mission, not the money. But once you understand how transferable your experience really is, everything changes.

1. Leadership That Translates

You already know what it's like to lead when the plan falls apart. That same steady hand you used in uniform is gold in business. The best entrepreneurs don't have all the answers; they just know how to lead people toward solutions.

That's exactly what you've done your entire career. Every squad, every briefing, every after-action review prepared you for managing projects, teams, and clients. Leadership is the bridge between your service and your success. You don't need to "learn business." You already know command.

2. Planning and Execution Under Fire

Most people crumble when pressure hits. You don't. That's because you were built for decisive action. A business owner without discipline is just guessing. But a veteran with a clear plan? That's a threat to the competition.

You've spent years creating order out of chaos, breaking down complex missions into step-by-step execution. That's the same muscle you'll use to run a business, scale a team, or manage investments.

You've already proven you can execute under fire. Now you're just doing it in a different arena, one that builds wealth instead of rank.

3. Adaptability and Resourcefulness

Every PCS, deployment, and leadership change taught you how to adjust fast. You know how to walk into an unfamiliar environment, assess it, and make it work. That ability to adapt quickly and stay mission-focused is the foundation of entrepreneurship.

Markets shift, trends change, plans collapse. The ones who survive are the ones who adjust without losing focus. Veterans don't wait for perfect conditions. We improvise, adapt, and overcome same principle, new battlefield.

4. The Mission Mindset

Here's the real difference between veterans and everyone else: purpose. You've never worked for a paycheck you've worked for a mission. And that's why you'll win. Because when business gets hard and it *will* get hard money won't be enough to keep most people going. But purpose will.

The same drive that made you serve your country is

the drive that will make you serve your clients, your community, and your future. Purpose makes profit sustainable.

5. Translating the Uniform to Ownership

The only real shift you have to make is this: You're no longer executing someone else's mission, you're writing your own. It's time to take all that leadership, discipline, adaptability, and strategy and point it toward your future.

You've already proven you can handle responsibility. Now it's about using those same systems to build freedom. That's the veteran advantage. You already have what everyone else is trying to find: structure, resilience, and a mission mindset. You just need to learn how to aim it.

The Bottom Line:

You're not starting from zero. You're starting from experience. You've already operated at a level most people can't imagine; now it's time to transfer that same intensity into your business and wealth strategy. The battlefield has changed, but the mission's the same: *Lead. Execute. Win.*

Chapter 2

Finding Your Purpose After Service

Leaving the military is like walking off the edge of a map. For years, every move you made was planned for you: orders, structure, chain of command. Then one day, it's gone. No formation. No mission brief. Just silence... and a question that hits every veteran sooner or later: *Now what?*

I know that feeling. You go from leading teams and managing millions in equipment to filling out job applications and trying to "fit in." It's not that you've lost your identity; it's that you haven't been asked to define it before. But here's the truth: you don't find purpose by accident. You build it, just like every other mission you've ever completed.

1. The Purpose Gap

Most veterans think they miss the *uniform*. What they really miss is the *mission*. In service, every day mattered. You knew what success looked like. You had a team, a goal, and a reason to push through. When that disappears, the gap isn't in rank; it's in direction.

That's why so many veterans struggle after transition. Not because they can't perform, but because they've lost the "why." The fix isn't to fill your schedule. It's to define your mission again this time, one that serves your family, your freedom, and your future.

2. Mission Redefined

Purpose doesn't have to look like combat or command. It just has to matter. Maybe your new mission is to build generational wealth. Maybe it's to create a business that hires veterans. Maybe it's to own property instead of renting for the rest of your life. Whatever it is, it has to be *yours*. Not what your peers are doing, not what recruiters say you should do. Your purpose after service is your chance to write your own op order, this time with your family's name at the top.

3. Rebuilding Your Identity

You're not "former" anything. You've evolved. You didn't lose value when you left the military; you gained options. But to use those options, you've got to stop defining yourself by what you *were* and start focusing on what you're *becoming*.

When you build a business, invest, or buy your first home, you're still serving. You're just serving in a new capacity: protecting your family, creating opportunities, and leading by example. That's leadership in its highest form.

4. Purpose Meets Profit

Here's the part nobody teaches you. Profit and purpose aren't enemies. They're allies. You don't have to feel guilty for wanting to build wealth. Money is just another resource that allows you to keep serving your family, your community, and other veterans coming up behind you. Purpose gives you direction. Profit gives you fuel. Together, they give you freedom.

5. The New Mission Statement

So what does your new mission look like? It might sound something like this: *"To create financial stability and opportunities for my family using the discipline, leadership, and strategy I learned in service."*

Simple. Clear. Actionable. You don't need a 20-page business plan, just a compass that keeps you moving toward freedom instead of survival.

The Bottom Line:

Purpose after service isn't found; it's designed. You've already proven you can live with discipline and direction. Now it's time to apply both to your future. You don't need permission to move forward. You just need to give yourself orders.

Chapter 3

Investing in Yourself

When I left the Army, I thought I was starting from scratch. No uniform. No rank. No mission brief, just me, a résumé, a DD-214, and no clue what came next. But here's what I didn't realize at the time: I wasn't broke. I was loaded — not with cash, but with benefits, experience, and leverage I hadn't learned to use yet. I didn't need to start over; I needed to activate what I already had.

1. Your Experience Is Equity

The military gives you more than discipline; it gives you economic value. Leadership, logistics, adaptability, systems thinking — that's consulting-level skill.

The problem is, most of us don't cash in because we don't translate what we did in uniform into civilian value.

Think about it: if you've led a platoon, you've managed a project. If you've maintained equipment, you've done asset management. If you've coordinated missions, you've handled logistics.

You already own transferable assets; they just need rebranding. The first investment you make after service should be learning how to communicate those skills in the language of the marketplace.

2. The G.I. Bill — Your First Business Grant

Too many veterans waste their education benefits chasing degrees that don't build wealth. The G.I. Bill isn't just for college; it's for positioning.

Want to start a business? Use it for certifications like project management, real estate, or IT. Want to invest in real estate? Use it for appraisal, inspection, or construction programs. Want to build a brand? Use it for business, marketing, or finance.

That's not "school." That's training to own your lane. If you don't use your G.I. Bill strategically, you're leaving tens of thousands of dollars and years of opportunity untouched.

3. SkillBridge: The Six-Month Business Internship

If you're still active duty and reading this, this section alone could change your transition forever.

SkillBridge allows you to spend the last 180 days of service training with a civilian company *while still getting your military paycheck*. That's not just an internship that's a soft launch into civilian entrepreneurship.

You can work under a small business owner, a real estate team, or even shadow an investor. That's six months of paid field training before you ever touch your savings or VA loan.

If you want to start your own business, *learn from someone already running one*. That's how you go from E-6 to CEO without skipping ranks.

4. COOL Programs — Get Certified on the Government's Dime

The DoD's COOL (Credentialing Opportunities On-Line) programs let you earn professional certifications paid for by Uncle Sam.

Electrician. Project manager. Personal trainer. Drone pilot. HVAC tech. It doesn't matter what your MOS was; there's a path to turn it into profit.

You can literally walk away from active duty with

credentials worth thousands, ready to work for yourself or step into a high-demand field. That's not just continuing education; that's preloaded entrepreneurship.

5. The VA's Hidden Entrepreneurship Tools

Most people think the VA just does healthcare. Wrong. They fund business ownership too. Through programs like the VA Small Business Program (VetBiz) and the Service-Disabled Veteran-Owned Small Business Certification, you can access government contracts and set your business up for *federal preference*.

In short: Civilian businesses compete. Veteran-owned businesses *get called first*. That's how you leverage your service beyond the uniform.

6. Compounding Through Experience

When you use your benefits strategically not emotionally every move compounds. Your G.I. Bill builds knowledge. Your SkillBridge builds experience. Your COOL certifications build credibility. Your VA business registration builds opportunity.

That's not random progress, that's a financial formation. Each benefit feeds the next until your service becomes self-sustaining wealth.

The Bottom Line

You didn't serve your country for 10, 15, or 20 years just to "start over." You've already paid the price now it's time to collect the return. Your benefits aren't handouts. They're *hand-ups*. They're launchpads to ownership if you use them right.

So before you spend a dollar trying to reinvent yourself, go claim the thousands already waiting for you. Because the next chapter *Finding Your Business Model* will show you how to put it all to work.

Chapter 4

Turning Experience into Income

When most people talk about "starting a business," they imagine Shark Tank pitches, fancy offices, and logos. That's noise. Real entrepreneurship starts smaller with awareness. You don't need a million-dollar idea. You just need to spot the problem you already know how to solve and build a system around it.

When I left the Army, I didn't start by looking for an idea. I started by looking at my experience. Thirteen years of logistics, leadership, and coordination. I didn't realize it yet, but I was sitting on a business model.

1. The First Business Plan is You

Forget the paperwork for a second. Your business model begins with your MOS. Every military role already fits into a civilian category.

- Mechanics become fleet or equipment-maintenance owners.
- Admin specialists become virtual assistants or operations consultants.
- Intel analysts become data strategists.
- Trainers become coaches.

The uniform changes, but the value doesn't. If you want to know what business to build, look at what people were already asking you for help with in the military. That's your market talking.

2. Mission Over Motion

When I first transitioned, I thought *motion = progress*. I registered an LLC, bought a logo, and made social media pages and then realized I didn't have a clear *mission*. That's the mistake most new entrepreneurs make. They build activity before clarity.

A mission answers three things:

1. Who am I helping?
2. What problem am I solving?
3. Why am I the one to solve it?

Everything else—website, marketing, even pricing—flows from that. If you can't write your mission on a Post-it, it's not clear enough yet.

3. Start with Proof, Not Perfection

You don't need to "launch;" you need to *validate*. Start testing your idea before you quit your job or spend your savings.

When I first got into real estate, I didn't build a full business plan. I started helping friends understand their VA loan. One conversation led to a referral, then a deal, then another. That's validation.

Every client you help and every problem you solve is market proof. Once people start paying for it, you refine it, document it, and scale it.

4. Use Your Benefits to Prototype

Here's the part most veterans miss: your benefits can *fund your first business idea.*

- Use your G.I. Bill to get a certification that supports it.
- Use SkillBridge to intern with a company already doing what you want to do.
- Use VA Small Business Programs or SBA Vet Advantage Loans for seed capital.

If you want to start a fitness brand, get certified while still on duty. If you want to run a trucking company, use COOL or SBA programs to get your CDL paid for. If you want to start a real estate or contracting business, SkillBridge under one before separation. That's not theory. That's taxpayer-funded incubation.

5. The Low-Cost Launch

Forget "Go big or go home." The real rule is "*Go lean and learn.*" You don't need a storefront. You need a client. You don't need employees. You need processes. You don't need an investor. You need momentum.

Use what's already free: social media, veteran networks, and LinkedIn. Pitch small. Deliver big. The first ten customers will teach you more than any business class ever could.

6. Scale After Sustainability

Too many vets chase growth before they build stability. They want a team, a brand, and a truck wrap before they've built consistent income. Build consistency first. That's your new "steady paycheck." Once your systems earn while you sleep, *then* expand. Scaling without sustainability is just chaos in nicer packaging.

The Bottom Line

You don't need a Silicon Valley idea to be successful; you need a soldier's mindset and a smart plan.

Start with what you know. Test before you invest. Use every benefit the government already gave you to turn your service into ownership.

You've executed missions far tougher than this. Now it's time to execute one that builds something lasting, a business that outlives your ETS date.

Chapter 5

Building Your Battle Plan

When you're in the military, no mission moves without a plan. You get your tasking order, identify your assets, and allocate resources before boots ever hit the ground. Business works the same way. The difference? No commander's coming to issue your operation order. This time, *you* write it. Your business battle plan starts with two missions: fund it and launch it.

1. Stop Waiting for Perfect Conditions

A lot of veterans stay stuck because they're waiting for everything to line up: the perfect business name, the perfect timing, and the perfect logo. Let me break it to you: that day doesn't come.

In the military, you never had "perfect intel." You had enough intel to act. That's what you need here enough to move forward.

When I first got into real estate, I didn't have a big

savings account or investors behind me. What I had was a plan, a network, and my benefits. You can build a business the same way by using what's already in your arsenal.

2. Fund the Mission Using Your Benefits

Let's start with money not from your pocket, but from your *earned leverage*. The government literally pays you to invest in yourself.

Here's how you use that to fund your next move:

- **The G.I. Bill:** Use it beyond degrees. Certifications, trade schools, project management, and business programs all qualify. Think bigger get the *credentials* that your customers will pay for.

- **Vocational Rehab (VR&E):** If you have a service-connected disability, this program can pay for training, equipment, and even *small-business startup tools*.

- **SBA Veterans Advantage Loans:** The Small Business Administration offers low-interest loans for vets with reduced fees. Use this for your first big equipment buy, a van, or startup costs.

- **VA Small Business Programs:** The VA has contracting and certification programs
  (SDVOSB/VOSB) that give veteran-owned businesses priority on federal contracts. That's not a
  handout, that's strategy.

You've already earned these benefits. You just haven't deployed them yet.

3. Build the War Chest — Without Going Broke

Cash flow is your ammo. Lose it too fast, and the
mission's over. You don't need a six-figure fund. You
need structure.

Start lean:

- **Separate your money.** Open a business check-
  ing account. Never mix personal and business
  funds.

- **Automate your budget.** Use tools like Quick-
  Books Self-Employed or Wave to track your
  spending.

- **Protect your credit.** Your credit score is your
  new clearance level and keep it mission ready.

Remember, the goal isn't to have money, it's to
have *control of your money.*

4. Strategic Allies and Joint Operations

In the field, you never ran a mission solo. You had intel, logistics, support, comms. Business is no different. You need a team not employees yet, but *alliances*.

Here's how you build your squad:

- **Mentors:** Find other veteran entrepreneurs. Learn from their mistakes.

- **Partners:** Link with people whose strengths fill your gaps marketers, accountants, web designers.

- **Lenders & Advisors:** Build relationships early. It's easier to ask for funding when they already know your mission.

Your network will open doors faster than your business plan ever will.

5. Test, Don't Guess

The best business plans are written *after* the first few transactions. Why? Because the market always gives feedback.

So, test early:

- Offer your service to a small audience.

- Ask for feedback before you scale.

- Fix what's broken before you invest more.

You don't need a thousand customers; you just need ten who believe in what you do and tell their friends.

6. Discipline > Motivation

You already know this from the military motivation fades, discipline lasts. You won't always feel like showing up for your business, but systems don't care about moods.

Set up habits:

- Designate a "business hour" every day, even if it's just one hour after work.

- Track your weekly objectives like you tracked training goals.

- Celebrate progress not perfection.

If you treat your business like a mission, it will reward you like a career.

The Bottom Line

You already know how to follow through on a plan.

You've executed complex missions with half the resources and twice the risk. Now it's time to turn that same discipline inward.

Use your benefits, your network, and your mindset to launch your business, not someday, but *this year*. Stop waiting for clearance. You're the commander now.

Chapter 6

The Transition Toolkit

When you're in uniform, structure isn't optional, it's built in. The Army gave you your schedule, your chain of command, and your mission. Once you hang up the uniform, that structure disappears overnight.

And that's why most veterans struggle in business. It's not because they're lazy or unmotivated. It's because the system that kept them sharp no longer exists. In the military, the system *creates* the discipline. In business, *you* have to create the system.

1. Build Your Battle Rhythm

Every successful business owner has a rhythm, a daily cadence that keeps operations tight even when things get hectic.

You already know this concept. PT, chow, formation every day, same time, no excuses. That consistency kept the machine running. Your business deserves the same energy.

Start with three anchors:

1. **Admin Day:** Handle finances, bookkeeping, and communications once a week.
2. **Execution Days:** The bulk of your week serving clients, producing, or selling.
3. **Planning Day:** Review wins, losses, and next week's objectives.

This is how you stop feeling "busy" and start being *productive.*

2. Automate or Die

If it can be automated, automate it. Manual tasks kill small businesses faster than competition ever will.

Here's the playbook:

- **Money Systems:** Use QuickBooks, Wave, or Notion to track income and expenses. Set alerts for late invoices.
- **Scheduling:** Calendly, Google Calendar, and automated text reminders save hours a week.

- **Customer Flow:** CRMs like HubSpot or HoneyBook can track leads, contracts, and follow-ups automatically.

The goal isn't to be everywhere, it's to build systems that *work when you don't.* That's how you buy back your freedom.

3. Find Your "Fire Team"

No one succeeds solo. Even when I was on deployment, success wasn't about who had rank, it was about who had your six.

In business, that team looks different but the principle's the same. Build your fire team around these four roles:

- **Mentor:** Someone who's already been where you're going.
- **Peer:** Another veteran or entrepreneur at your same stage accountability keeps you sharp.
- **Advisor:** Your tax or legal expert. Not exciting, but vital.
- **Support:** The family or friend who reminds you *why* you're doing this when things get tough.

This team will keep you grounded when you start feeling like you're losing the mission.

4. Stay Mentally Fit for the Fight

Let's be real entrepreneurship is isolation mixed with adrenaline. You'll have weeks where business is booming, followed by weeks when you're questioning everything. You can't avoid the grind, but you can manage it.

Here's how:

- **Keep a routine**. Sleep, meals, workouts the basics matter.
- **Check your circle**. Spend time with people who push, not drain, you.
- **Use your resources**. VA and Vet Centers offer counseling and business coaching for free use them.
- **Remember your "why."** Write it down and keep it visible.

You trained your body for combat, now train your mind for creation.

5. Don't Chase, Build

A lot of vets get caught in the "hustle" mindset. They're chasing every lead, every opportunity, every dollar. That's survival mode not strategy.

In the service, you didn't chase targets; you executed plans. Business works the same way. Focus on building systems not just sales. Systems create sustainability, and sustainability creates wealth. You don't want to stay in hustle mode forever. You want a machine that grows without burning you out.

6. Remember: You're Not Starting Over

This part's personal. When I left the Army, I thought I was back at zero. No rank, no command, no structure. But here's what I eventually realized you're never starting over. You're starting *from experience*.

You've led missions, managed chaos, and built teams under pressure that most civilians will never understand. That's not a disadvantage, that's your edge.

The same systems that helped you succeed in the Army can build your business today. You just have to rewire them for freedom instead of formation.

The Bottom Line

Success doesn't come from working harder, it comes from building smarter. Structure equals freedom. Systems equal scalability. If you treat your business like a mission, it will reward you like one.

You already know how to adapt, overcome, and execute. Now you just have to apply it to your next objective—*sustained success*. Stay disciplined. Stay strategic. Stay in the fight.

Chapter 7

The Transition Trap

When I left the Army, I thought the hardest part would be finding my next paycheck. It wasn't. The hardest part was finding *my new rhythm.*

In the military, purpose is built into your day. In entrepreneurship, you have to build it yourself and if you're not careful, you'll burn out before your business even breaks even.

There are three traps that catch almost every new veteran entrepreneur: the mental trap, the financial trap, and the social trap.

1. The Mental Trap — Trading One Uniform for Another

The first thing I tell veterans who start a business: Be careful not to become your own bad boss. When we transition, we crave control but what most of us really build is *a job disguised as a business.*

We work longer hours, take fewer breaks, and demand more from ourselves than any commander ever did. That's not freedom. That's fatigue in civilian clothing. Your business can't depend on your burnout. Build it around systems, not stamina.

And mentally? Give yourself permission to slow down. You've been running on military tempo for years. Now your mission is endurance not just performance.

Ask Antwaun Tip:
Structure your work week like a deployment rotation. Plan rest days, recovery time, and personal "mission pauses."

Because burnout doesn't make you a better leader it just makes you unavailable when it counts.

2. The Financial Trap — Confusing Cash Flow with Profit

Here's where most new entrepreneurs fall flat: They think making money equals keeping money. You can have a business doing $100,000 a year and still be broke. I've seen it too many times great operators who never separate income from expenses, and by tax season, they're upside down. Remember: cash flow is oxygen, but profit is life.

Keep three accounts from day one:

1. **Operating Account:** Where money comes in and expenses go out.

2. **Tax Account:** 20–25% of every payment gets set aside. No exceptions.

3. **Profit Account:** Even if it's 5%, you pay your business first not last.

That's your new pay structure. You don't work for the business; the business works for you.

Ask Antwaun Tip:
The government gives veterans access to small-business financial mentors through the *SBA Boots to Business* and *VETRN* programs, free training that can keep you from blowing up your balance sheet before you scale.

---

3. The Social Trap — The Wrong Circle, The Wrong Counsel

When you get out, your circle changes and not always for the better. Some friends won't understand what you're building. Others will think you've "changed." And truthfully? You have. You're shifting from earning to *creating*. That's a mindset few people get. So stop expecting everyone to understand it.

The real danger comes when you take advice from people who've never built anything. If you want business advice, ask entrepreneurs not employees. If you want financial growth, ask investors not spenders. Guard your circle like you guarded your unit. You can't take every friend to the next mission.

Ask Antwaun Tip:
Surround yourself with growth-
minded veterans.

There are veteran entrepreneur networks, SBA cohorts, and private Facebook groups built for this where people actually talk systems, funding, and strategy instead of complaining about the VA.

4. The Invisible Trap — Losing Yourself in the Hustle

There's one more trap no one warns you about: success without identity. When your business finally starts working, you'll be tempted to make it your whole identity your new uniform. Don't.

Your value isn't tied to your title or your revenue. You served your country. You built something from scratch. You've already proven yourself. Now the goal is balance, building without breaking.

The Bottom Line

The mission isn't just to build a business. It's to build one that doesn't break *you*. You've already done hard things. You've already learned how to endure. Now, the challenge is to learn how to sustain mentally, financially, and socially.

Don't fall into the traps. Stay disciplined, stay grounded, and remember: Freedom isn't earned through hustle. It's earned through alignment when your purpose, your systems, and your peace all move in the same direction.

Chapter 8

The Power of Partnerships

When I left the military, I thought being a business owner meant doing everything myself. I'd earned my independence, and I guarded it like it was a clearance level. But that's the problem.

Most veterans trade one chain of command for another. This time, it's self-imposed. We try to be the CEO, the accountant, the marketer, and the janitor all in one. And before long, we realize freedom without support feels a lot like isolation.

The truth is the same reason your missions succeeded in the military, the *team* is the same reason your business will succeed now.

1. You Don't Lose Strength by Sharing It

The best leaders I ever had weren't the ones who barked orders; they were the ones who empowered others to perform. Business isn't about control; it's about collaboration. You can't scale if you don't trust anyone else to hold the rope.

When I first started in real estate, I tried doing it all: showings, paperwork, marketing, client calls, and contracts. And guess what? I burned out. It wasn't until I started partnering with people—lenders, inspectors, and other agents that my business actually grew. Partnership doesn't make you weaker. It multiplies your reach.

2. Know the Difference Between Allies and Attachments

Not everyone you meet in business deserves to be in your formation. An *ally* adds value they bring something you don't have. An *attachment* drains value they take your energy and slow your pace.

You'll know the difference quickly:

- Allies help you execute.
- Attachments need to be convinced.

The military taught you to recognize weak links. The same applies here. Build with people who show up with the same mission-first mindset those who talk less about "what they want" and more about "how we win."

3. Divide the Work, Multiply the Win

You know how a unit functions: every MOS has a purpose. If everyone tries to be the squad leader, nothing moves. Your business works the same way.

One person's the strategist, another's the operator, another's the face of the brand. When everyone leans into their lane, the mission moves faster.

That's not delegation, that's deployment. You're assigning strengths to where they'll do the most good. And when the win comes, it's shared. That's the culture you build not competition, but cohesion.

4. Don't Confuse Independence with Isolation

When you first go solo, it feels good to call all the shots. But over time, you start realizing something's missing. In the military, you had brothers and sisters-in-arms people who understood the grind, the pressure, the purpose. In entrepreneurship, that connection has to be rebuilt.

Find your squad. Join veteran networking groups, small-business meetups, or mastermind circles. Talk with other builders who understand what it feels like to be responsible for everything.

Because the truth is isolation is quiet failure. You

stop learning, you stop growing, and you start believing that no one gets it. But there's a whole community that does. You just have to show up for it.

5. Partnerships Don't Just Build Business — They Build Balance

When you start working with the right people, something powerful happens. You stop trying to out-work the clock and start working in alignment.

Your partners keep you accountable, grounded, and honest. They remind you why you started. They challenge you to think bigger. That's when business stops feeling like survival and starts feeling like purpose again.

6. The Leadership Lesson Never Changes

The rank on your chest may be gone, but the principle stays the same: *lead from the front, not from above.* In business, leadership isn't about authority; it's about example.

Be the one who communicates clearly, pays fairly, and honors commitments. When you operate with integrity, you attract the same kind of people. And that's how real partnerships form—not from contracts, but from character.

The Bottom Line

You don't have to build alone. You didn't climb the ranks alone, and you won't grow a lasting business alone either. Partnerships are the multiplier effect of success. They turn one person's dream into a team's reality.

Find your allies. Protect your energy. Build with people who understand the mission. That's how you move from surviving to thriving, from "I" to "we."

Chapter 9

Golden Nuggets

Tactical lessons and mindset reminders to keep your mission sharp.

Every mission ends with a debrief. This is yours. Building a business after the military isn't about starting over it's about *translating* what you already know into new terrain.

You already understand discipline, systems, and accountability. You've executed under pressure, led teams, and solved problems with limited resources. Business isn't foreign to you. It's just a new theater of operations.

Here are the takeaways, the lessons worth carrying forward:

1. Your Skills Are Transferable — Use Them
You didn't lose your edge when you turned in your uniform; you just need to repurpose it.

Leadership becomes management. Operational planning becomes business strategy. After-action reviews become performance metrics.

2. Freedom Without Structure Is Chaos

Every successful entrepreneur runs a system whether it's a marketing calendar or a financial checklist. Structure doesn't limit freedom; it *protects* it. Build routines, track metrics, and plan your downtime like missions.

3. Purpose Beats Profit Every Time

Money comes and goes; mission stays. If your "why" isn't strong, the first setback will take you out. Build around service, helping others, solving problems, and creating value. That's the kind of mission that lasts.

4. Partnerships Multiply Power

Success is never solo. Find allies who complement your skills and share your values. Partnership isn't about dividing profit, it's about multiplying potential.

5. Adaptation Is the New Discipline

The battlefield changes. So does the market. Don't get attached to the way things were. Get attached to winning even if it means pivoting the plan.

6. Your Business Should Work for You

If you can't step away for a week without everything falling apart, you built a cage, not a company. Document systems. Train replacements. Automate what you can. Freedom is the ROI of smart systems.

7. Invest in Your Mindset Before Your Marketing

Confidence is the first product you sell to yourself. Before you convince customers, convince yourself your experience matters. Because it does.

8. Fail Forward — and Fail Fast

In the military, mistakes get corrected in real time. In business, most people freeze. They sit in analysis mode, trying to perfect the plan before they move and that hesitation costs them everything.

When I launched my first venture, half my ideas didn't land. I spent money on things that didn't convert, tried systems that didn't stick, and trusted people who didn't deliver. But every failure taught me something I couldn't learn from a webinar.

You have to fail *forward* and fail *fast*. Don't stall trying to make your first move perfect. Your goal isn't perfection, it's progression. Because business, like battle, rewards momentum. If you're always learning, you're never really losing.

9. You're Never Alone in the Fight

There's a community of veterans building, creating, and winning right now. Connect with them. Share resources. Trade intel. Iron sharpens iron but only if it's in contact.

10. Discipline Creates Freedom

That's the ultimate nugget. Freedom isn't built by shortcuts; it's built by structure, sacrifice, and consistency. You've lived that already. Now apply it to your business, your family, your finances, and your future.

The Bottom Line

This isn't the end of your mission; it's the relaunch. Every tool, lesson, and principle in this book is a weapon in your arsenal. Use them. Test them. Refine them. Because success after service isn't about what you lost; it's about what you learned. And you've already been trained for this.

So gear up, step out, and execute. The next chapter

of your life doesn't start when you're ready; it starts when you *move*.

Epilogue

The Next Mission

When the uniform comes off, the mission doesn't end. It just changes shape. For years, we've been trained to complete the mission, protect the team, and execute the plan, no excuses.

But once the military chapter closes, too many of us forget that those same principles still apply. The only difference now is the objective.

Your new mission isn't deployment; it's development. Not for the country this time but for yourself, your family, and your legacy. The battlefield becomes the business field. The mission brief becomes a business plan. And the reward isn't a medal; it's ownership, freedom, and impact.

I've seen too many brothers and sisters in arms trade their potential for comfort. They separate with leadership, work ethic, and discipline but never apply them to building wealth or independence.

The truth is, you don't need to start over. You just need to *reposition* your skills. You've already proven you can follow orders. Now it's time to write your own. The blueprint is here. The tools are in your hands. And the mission clock is running.

The next move is yours. If you're ready to stop surviving transitions and start *strategizing* them, if you're ready to take the same structure that got you through service and use it to create real freedom, then it's time to put your plan in motion.

About The Author

 Antwaun Hill is a U.S. Army veteran and Hawaii-based real estate professional who's helped countless military families turn their benefits into wealth.

After serving 13 years in the Army and another decade as a Department of Defense contractor, he discovered a truth that changed his life: "Financial freedom isn't earned through rank; it's built through strategy."

Through his brand Ask Antwaun, he's become a leading voice in VA loan education, teaching service members how to leverage BAH, entitlement, and PCS cycles to build equity, ownership, and legacy.

His "BAH Means Buy A House" movement has inspired thousands to stop renting, start investing, and take control of their financial missions.

When he's not helping families navigate homeownership or writing his next guide, you'll find him mentoring fellow veterans, spending time with his family, and building his own legacy one property at a time.

Need real estate answers? Just Ask Antwaun.
AskAntwaun@gmail.com

Other books in this series